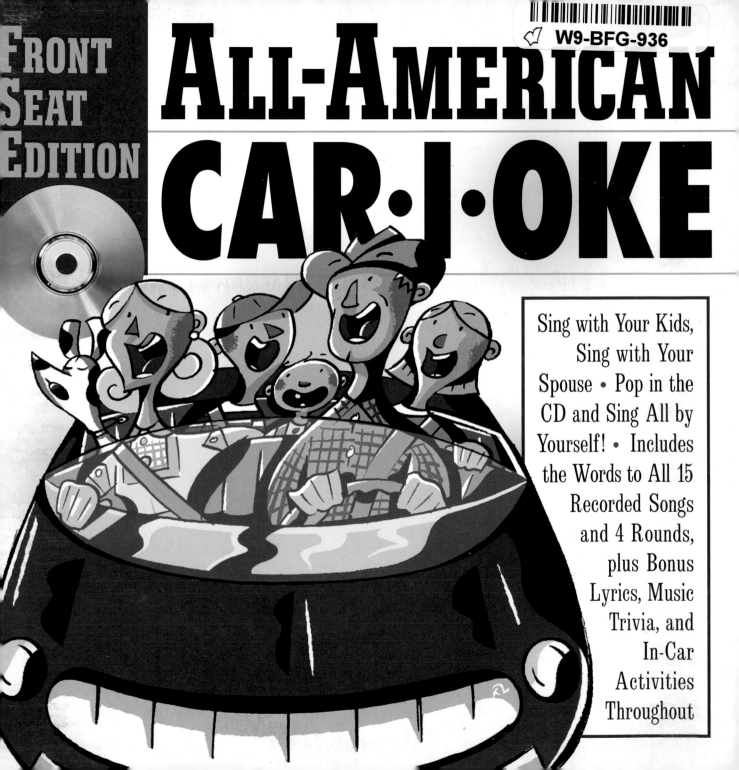

ALL-AMERICAN CAR·J·OKE

FRONT SEAT EDITION

W9-BFG-936

Sing with Your Kids, Sing with Your Spouse • Pop in the CD and Sing All by Yourself! • Includes the Words to All 15 Recorded Songs and 4 Rounds, plus Bonus Lyrics, Music Trivia, and In-Car Activities Throughout

ALL-AMERICAN
CAR·I·OKE

David Schiller

WORKMAN PUBLISHING · NEW YORK

For Asa, who knows all the words,
and the backseat singers: Quinn, Theo, and Clara.

Published simultaneously in Canada
by Thomas Allen & Son Limited.

Library of Congress Cataloging-in-Publication Data
All-American Car-i-oke / by David Schiller.
p. cm.
Includes 3 booklets of lyrics.
ISBN 0-7611-3068-3 (alk. paper)
1. Songs, English—United States—Texts. 2. Games for travelers.
I. Title: All-American Carioke. II. Schiller, David. III. Title.

M1628.A55 2003
782.42164'026'8—dc21   2003042282

Workman books are available at special discounts when
purchased in bulk for premiums and sales promotions
as well as for fund-raising or educational use.
Special editions or book excerpts can also be created to specification.
For details, contact the Special Sales Director at the address below.

Workman Publishing Company
708 Broadway
New York, NY 10003-9555
www.workman.com

Printed in China

First printing: June 2003

10 9 8 7 6 5 4 3 2 1

CONTENTS

A-One and a-Two and a. v

When the Saints Go Marching In 1

Proud Mary. 4

Dancing with Your Seat Belt On 7

The Big Rock Candy Mountains 8

Sloop John B. 12

All in the Family. 16

Mama Don't Allow 18

Day-O (Banana Boat Song) 20

Aye, Mateys! 23

Backseat Boogie-Woogie 24

Cielito Lindo 26

Rise and Shine 28

Gospel Sing-along 32

The Star-Spangled Banner 34

An Americana Song Sampler 36

The City of New Orleans 38

Planes, Trains, and Automobiles 41

Red River Valley 42

Gather 'Round the Campfire 44

Give My Regards to Broadway. 46

Danny Boy 48

Are We There Yet Blues 50

Round and Round. 54

Acknowledgments, Credits, and Big Thanks 56

WELCOME TO CARIOKE

A-ONE AND A-TWO AND A . . .

TRACK 1

Turn your car into an old-fashioned family parlor with the radio as a player piano. ALL-AMERICAN CAR-I-OKE combines a sweet old tradition—the family sing-along—with the new, a variation of karaoke. The result is a trip in the car where everyone comes together in activity and song.

After all, next to the shower, there's no better place for singing than the car. But even for families who make a habit of singing while driving, there are always two obstacles: getting everyone to agree on what songs to sing, and having everyone know the words.

Carioke is a takeoff of karaoke, the international phenomenon that started in Japan in the 1970s. Of course, carioke is not quite as sophisticated as today's karaoke—a book and booklets deliver the words instead of a video screen. But the basic idea is the same: singers are given a recorded backup track, and complete lyrics are provided. And ALL-AMERICAN CAR-I-OKE has something that karaoke doesn't—a book's worth of activities, information, trivia, and lore. It's not just a collection of songs, it's a whole musical enterprise.

But back to those songs. What to include? How to choose? Contemporary Top 40 or golden oldies? Broadway show tunes or childhood campfire tunes? Beatles or Stones—or neither? (Actually, neither!) In the end, ALL-AMERICAN CAR-I-OKE offers a selection of easy-to-sing, family-friendly favorites, familiar enough that most of us know them already, at least by melody.

"Empty Orchestra"

Legend has it that when a strolling guitarist couldn't make it to his gig at a snack bar in Kobe, Japan, the enterprising owner prepared tapes of accompaniment recordings and the patrons sang along. This was in the late 1970s. Karaoke—which means "empty orchestra" in Japanese—was born. It quickly spread throughout the rest of Japan, and just as quickly around the globe. New technologies have made karaoke ever more accessible (affordable home machines, for example) and also more sophisticated, with nifty developments

Breathe Like a Singer

Good breath control is to a singer what good bowing technique is to a violinist. Here are four simple rules for breathing while singing:

1. Lift your ribs and keep them up throughout the song.

2. Breathe deeply.

3. Keep your throat open and chin relaxed. To know what an open throat feels like, concentrate on the feeling you have the next time you yawn—but just before you open your mouth.

4. Whenever possible, take a breath at least a beat before you start to sing.

The music on the CD was arranged and recorded in Nashville. The aim was to provide friendly, energetic accompaniment. The result is something greater—instrumental tracks that are a pleasure to listen to even when not singing. Just play the first music track, "When the Saints Go Marching In." It swings.

But it's even better when you're singing along, and that's the heart of it. The thing to do is to take a deep breath and just plunge right in. As in karaoke, inhibitions disappear and the joy of singing takes over. Remember, it's not about singing in perfect pitch or seeing who can give the better performance. It's about having fun together. And this is where you can get creative. Some songs beg to be sung in harmony, others by one voice, and others want a lead and backup. Have fun arranging the family! You can play with diction and tone; you can belt it out or whisper; pronounce every syllable or hold the vowels and add a quaver; even put on funny accents. Occasional vocal cues will help you find  your way through a song. There's also an introductory CD track (track 1: How to Carioke) that gives useful pointers on how to carioke.

More songs are included in the book than are recorded on the CD. These extras are for when the mood strikes, and most of them have very well-known melodies. The feeling was that one can never have enough songs. That's just how it is when you start singing— once you get going, you're not going to want to stop.

like the ability to transpose the music's key to suit the singer's voice. Karaoke is a worldwide phenomenon, flirting with professionalism (clubs, competitions) while retaining its irrepressibly charming amateur spirit.

ALL TOGETHER NOW

WHEN THE SAINTS GO MARCHING IN

TRACK ❷

Join the band and get ready to swing! This gospel song, written in the late 1800s by James M. Black with lyrics by Katherine Purvis, leaped into the American consciousness when Louis Armstrong recorded it for Decca in 1938. (This recording, by the way, was named as one of the "365 Songs of the Century" by the Recording Industry Association of America and National Endowment for the Arts.) Other well-known versions belong to Al Hirt, Mahalia Jackson, and The Weavers. But it's Satchmo you'll hear in our New Orleans–style arrangement. Listen for the big hole after the intro, and then come in on top of it. And no matter whether the sun is beginning to shine or refusing to shine, this song is about the pure joy of being "in that number."

WHEN THE SAINTS GO MARCHING IN

Chorus:
Oh, when the saints *(Oh, when the saints)*
Go marching in *(Go marching in)*
Oh, when the saints go marching in
Yes, I want to be in that number
When the saints go marching in.

QUICK! CHECK THAT BOX OF OLD LPS IN THE ATTIC!

Here's a great trivia question: What was the first commercial record released that the Beatles played on? That's right, it was Tony Sheridan's *MyBonnie / The Saints* ("When the Saints Go Marching In"). It was first released in Germany in 1961, then in the U.K. on January 5, 1962, then in the U.S. in April 1962. These songs were also part of the first commercial LP

First verse (trombone accompaniment):
And when the sun
Refuse to shine
Oh, when the sun refuse to shine
Yes, I want to be in that number
When the sun refuse to shine.

Chorus:
Oh, when the saints *(Oh, when the saints)*
Go marching in *(Go marching in)*
Oh when the saints go marching in
Yes, I want to be in that number
When the saints go marching in.

Instrumental

Second verse (saxophone accompaniment):
Oh, when the trumpet
Sounds a call
Oh, when the trumpet sounds a call
Yes, I want to be in that number
When the trumpet sounds a call.

Third verse (guitar accompaniment):
Oh, when we all
Clap hands and sing
Oh, when we all
Clap hands and sing
Yes, I want to be in that number
When we all clap hands and sing.

Chorus/finale:
Oh, when the saints *(Oh, when the saints)*
Go marching in *(Go marching in)*
Oh, when the saints go marching in
Yes, I want to be in that number
When the saints go marching in.

to feature the Beatles by name. Called *My Bonnie,* the Tony Sheridan album—with a little asterisked copy on the back that says, "Accompanied by the Beatles"—is all but impossible to find. By the way, the drummer for the Beatles was Pete Best.

PROUD MARY

TRACK ③

"Proud Mary" is a tale of two interpretations. In 1968, Creedence Clearwater Revival released it as a straightforward rock tune, and it became their international breakthrough, topping the U.S. charts at #2 and the U.K. charts at #8. Three years later, Ike and Tina Turner transformed "Proud Mary" into an electrifying rhythm and blues opus that teasingly begins "nice and easy" but promises to "do the finish rough." Explosive is more like it. It won the Grammy that year for best R&B Vocal Performance by a Group. Our version starts slow, then rocks. Find your inner Tina, and let loose. And for those in the car who can make like Ike, see how deep you can go with a bassy "Rollin'" counterpoint.

PROUD MARY

Words and music by John Fogerty © 1968 Jondora Music (BMI).
All rights reserved. Used by permission.

Intro:
Rollin' *(Rollin')*, Rollin' *(Rollin')*,
Rollin' on a river.

First verse:
Left a good job in the city
Workin' for the man every night and day
But I never lost one minute of sleeping
Worried about the way things might have been.

4

Chorus:

Big wheel keep on turnin',
Proud Mary keep on burnin',
Rollin' *(Rollin')*, Rollin' *(Rollin')*,
Rollin' on a river.

Second verse:

Cleaned a lot of plates in Memphis,
Pumped a lot of pain in New Orleans,
But I never saw the good side of the city,
Until I hitched a ride on a river boat queen.

Chorus:

Big wheel keep on turnin',
Proud Mary keep on burnin',
Rollin' *(Rollin')*, Rollin' *(Rollin')*,
Rollin' on a river.
Rollin' *(Rollin')*, Rollin' *(Rollin')*,
Rollin' on a river.

Now speed way up!

driving three-minute songs featuring John Fogerty's growling, Cajun-inflected vocals. In 1969, they were Billboard's Top Singles Artists and performed on the second highest bill at Woodstock. By October, 1972, they had officially disbanded.

ROLL OVER, BEETHOVEN

What makes a great song? How about just two notes? Believe it or not, John Fogerty was playing around with the famous introduction to Beethoven's Fifth Symphony—the one that begins, Ba-ba-ba-BAH—and shortened it to Ba-BAH, Ba-BAH. And "Proud Mary" was off and running. By the way, he also thought the riff sounded like the wheel at the back of a boat, which led to the subject of the song.

Repeat first verse:
Left a good job in the city,
Workin' for the man every night and day,
But I never lost one minute of sleeping,
Worried about the way things might have been.

Chorus:
Big wheel keep on turnin' *(Turnin')*,
Proud Mary keep on burnin' *(Burnin')*,
Rollin' *(Rollin')*, Rollin' *(Rollin')*,
Rollin' on a river.
Rollin' *(Rollin')*, Rollin' *(Rollin')*,
Rollin' on a river.

Third verse:
If you come down to the river,
I betcha you're gonna find some people who live.
You don't have to worry 'cause you have no money,
People along the river are happy to give.

Repeat chorus

DANCING WITH YOUR SEAT BELT ON

All right, so Ed Sullivan isn't watching (explain this one to your kids), you're not wearing color-coordinated outfits, *and* you're sitting down! Don't let that stop you from finding a groove. Try these moves to go with your singing.

Big wheel keep on turnin',
Twirl finger over head. (Repeat)

Proud Mary keeps on burnin'.
Pump fist up and down. (Repeat)

Rollin', (Rollin'), Rollin', (Rollin'),
Roll arms up and down with hands in fists. (Repeat)

For a finesse move, jerk thumb over shoulder at the end of the roll.

Rollin' on a river.
Move arms and hands in a riverlike fashion.

ROLLING ON THE RIVER

No, there was no riverboat named *Proud Mary*. In fact, John Fogerty thought up the title long before he knew what his song was to going be about. But during most of the nineteenth century and into the twentieth, paddlewheel riverboats plied America's inland rivers, hauling people and goods. Probably the best-known account is Mark Twain's *Life on the Mississippi*, the classic memoir of his years as a cub pilot.

THE BIG ROCK CANDY MOUNTAINS

TRACK 4

This classic hobo ballad resurfaced in a big way through an immensely popular and influential soundtrack, the Grammy-winning *O Brother, Where Art Thou?* Featuring both original recordings—like Harry "Haywire Mac" McClintock's 1928 version of "The Big Rock Candy Mountains"—and contemporary artists reaching back, *O Brother* introduced a whole new generation of listeners to American roots music. Sometimes funny, sometimes dark, often plaintive and always raw, roots music is worlds away from the slick commercial pop that dominates the airwaves today. There's a reason it's called roots—it's where rock, folk, country, R&B, and even hip-hop got their start.

The carioke version of "The Big Rock Candy Mountains" tweaks the lyrics here and there to give it a more contemporary spin. But then again, reinterpretation is all part of the roots tradition, too.

THE BIG ROCK CANDY MOUNTAINS
Words and music by Harry McClintock, new lyrics by David Schiller.

Intro:

On a summer's day in the month of May,
A third-grader come a-boarding,
Coasting along that lonesome road
To a place much more rewarding.
He said, "I'm headed for a land that's far away,
Beside them crystal fountains—
So come with me
We'll go and see
the Big Rock Candy Mountains."

First verse:

In the Big Rock Candy Mountains
You never change your socks,
And little streams of Mountain Dew
Come a-trickling down the rocks.
You're stoked on all the banks and ramps,
And life is one big jam,
There's a Slurpy lake with nachos, too,
You can paddle all around 'em in a big canoe
In the Big Rock Candy Mountains.

the Lone Prairie." In 1938, "Haywire Mac" set off for Hollywood, where fortune smiled on him, and he kept busy playing villains in Gene Autry and Durango Kid movies. When he wasn't lucky enough to get an active bad-guy part, he was often the one who stood there to say, "He went thataway!"

WORKERS OF THE WORLD, UNITE— IN SONG

In addition to his many other lives, Harry McClintock was once a singer who rallied the Wobblies, the fabled union of Big Bill Haywood, Mother Jones, and Joe Hill. Officially the I.W.W.— International Workers of the World—the Wobblies were a radical but short-lived group formed in 1905 with the aim of organizing unskilled workers into "one big union" that would wrest control away from bosses. With every union card came a little red songbook. Pete Seeger called them "the singingest union America ever had."

Second verse:
In the Big Rock Candy Mountains,
There's a land that's fair and bright,
Where the Gameboys grow on bushes
And you hang out every night;
Where little brothers stay out of your way
And little sisters too,
Oh, I'm bound to go,
Where I can catch any show,
The alarm never rings
And my father never sings,
In the Big Rock Candy Mountains.

Third verse:
In the Big Rock Candy Mountains
Classrooms are made of tin
And you can bust right out again
As soon as they put you in;
The teachers show up just once a week
To hand out nothing but A's,
Oh, I'm going to stay
Where you sleep all day,
Where they slammed the jerk
Who invented homework
In the Big Rock Candy Mountains.

Fourth verse:
In the Big Rock Candy Mountains
You can burp right after you eat,
And never have to brush your teeth,
And forget about being neat;
You can throw your clothes all over the floor,
Eat candy in your bed.
Oh, that's the life for me,
Completely parent-free,
Where your only job
Is to act like a slob,
In the Big Rock Candy Mountains.

Finale:
And so now my song is over,
I'm lacing up my Vans,
I'm pointing my board
To the open road
Where the bluebirds sing
And kids are king
In the Big Rock Candy Mountains.

SLOOP JOHN B.

TRACK 5

This breezy island song comes from the neighborhood of Nassau Town in the Bahamas. A comical adventure of life aboard a ship, "Sloop John B." showed up as "The John B. Sails" in Carl Sandburg's landmark 1927 folk collection, *The American Songbag*. The Weavers adapted and arranged it as "The Wreck of John B." And then came the Beach Boys. Planted smack in the middle of their hugely influential album, *Pet Sounds* (1966), "Sloop John B." charted at #3 and has since appeared in dozens of compilations, including the soundtrack for *Forrest Gump*.

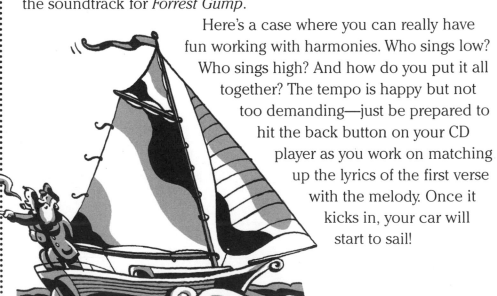

Here's a case where you can really have fun working with harmonies. Who sings low? Who sings high? And how do you put it all together? The tempo is happy but not too demanding—just be prepared to hit the back button on your CD player as you work on matching up the lyrics of the first verse with the melody. Once it kicks in, your car will start to sail!

Sloop John B.

Introduction:

I want to go ho-o-o-o-me!
I feel so broke up,
I want to go home!

First verse:

Oh, we come on the sloop John B.,
My grandfather and me,
Around Nassau Town we did roam.
Singing all night,
Got into a fight,
Well, I feel so broke up,
I want to go home!

Chorus:

So—
Hoist up the John B. sails.
See how the mainsail sets.
Call for the captain ashore,
Let me go home!
Let me go home!
I want to go ho-o-o-o-me!
Feel so broke up,
I want to go home!

wedged in by the record company because it was the group's current hit single. The song may sound out of place, but it has some of the most gorgeous male harmonies ever heard on any rock record.

THE WHAT JOHN B.?

A **sloop** is a type of sailboat with a single mast that's set toward the front of the boat. Other general styles of sailboats include the **cutter**— with a single mast set in the boat's middle. The **schooner**—with two or more masts, in which the main mast is set behind the smaller mast(s). **Catamaran**— a sailboat with two hulls. The **ketch** and **yawl** are boats with two masts, but the steering wheel of the ketch is between the masts.

Second verse:
First mate got in a funk,
Broke in the captain's trunk.
The constable had to come and
    take him away.
Sheriff John Stone,
Why don't you leave me alone?
Well, I feel so broke up
I want to go home!

Chorus:
So—
Hoist up the John B. sails.
See how the mainsail sets.
Call for the captain ashore,
Let me go home!
Let me go home!
Ho-o-o-o-me!
Feel so broke up,
I want to go home!

Third verse:

The poor cook he got the fits,
Threw away all the grits,
And then he took and he ate up
    all of my corn.
Let me go home,
Why don't they let me go home!
This is the worst trip—
I've ever been on!

Chorus/finale:

So—
Hoist up the John B. sails.
See how the mainsail sets.
Call for the captain ashore,
Let me go home!
Let me go home!
Ho-o-o-o-me!
Feel so broke up,
I want to go home.
I want to go—ho-o-o-o-me!
Feel so broke up,
I want to go home.

ALL IN THE FAMILY

Sing just one song together, in the car or elsewhere, and you join in a tradition that goes back centuries: families making music together. Some of the most renowned include:

THE BACHS The great Baroque composer and organist Johann Sebastian Bach learned basic music theory as well as how to play the harp and violin from his father, a town musician. Notable among Bach's many musical children are Carl Philipp Emanuel Bach, harpsichordist to Frederick the Great of Prussia, and Wilhelm Friedemann Bach, organist and composer of music for organ, piano, orchestra, and small ensembles.

THE VON TRAPPS Known to millions through the movie *The Sound of Music*, the Von Trapps—Captain Von Trapp, his wife Maria, and their ten children, Rupert, Agathe, Maria, Werner, Hedwig, Johanna, Martina, Rosmarie, Lorli, and Johannes—began singing professionally after they fled Austria in 1938. A tour of America led them to Stowe, Vermont, where they founded the Trapp Family Music Camp and Trapp Family Lodge.

THE JACKSONS Joseph and Katherine Jackson of Gary, Indiana, had nine children, and the rest is pop history. First came the Billboard-topping Jackson 5, consisting of brothers Jackie, Tito, Jermaine, Marlon, and Michael. Then parallel solo careers for Jackie, Jermaine, and Michael. Then a 1970s TV variety show introducing the sisters, Rebbie, LaToya, and Janet. Then Michael Jackson's *Thriller*, bestselling album of all time. And now Janet.

THE CARTER-CASH FAMILY They were the first family of country music: A. P. Carter, his wife, Sarah, and Sarah's cousin Maybelle. The legacy continued as Maybelle toured with her daughters, June, Helen and Anita, and along the way met·up with an edgy young country singer named Johnny Cash, who went on to chart more than 100 country hits. Johnny married June, and together they raised two famous musician daughters, Rosanne Cash and Carlene Carter.

Other notable musical families:

THE MAMAS AND THE PAPAS

Among the original members were husband and wife John Phillips and Michelle Phillips. Their daughter, Chynna, joined Beach Boy Brian Wilson's daughters Carnie and Wendy to form Wilson Phillips.

THE BEACH BOYS

A true family act, consisting of brothers Brian, Dennis, and Carl Wilson with cousin Mike Love (and nonfamily member Al Jardine).

THE MARLEYS •

Reggae star Bob Marley reached international fame before dying of brain cancer at thirty-six. Among his children are Ziggy, Stephen, Sharon, and Cedella, who play together as the Melody Makers, and Stephen, Rohan, Julian, and Damian, who are the Ghetto Youths.

THE MARSALISES

It's a jazz dynasty: father Ellis and sons Wynton, Branford, Delfeayo, and Jason.

THE JUDDS

Mother Naomi and daughter Wynonna had fourteen #1 country hits. Another daughter, Ashley, is a movie star.

Other musical combinations include brothers and sisters, husbands and wives, parents and children. Here are some partial lists. Can you think of others?

SIBLING BANDS

Everly Brothers	Bee Gees
Allman Brothers	Roches
Carpenters	McGarrigle Sisters
Osmonds	Neville Brothers
Pointer Sisters	Credence Clearwater Revival

MUSICAL HUSBANDS AND WIVES

(kids in the backseat, take note!)
Sonny and Cher
Les Paul and Mary Ford
Roy Rogers and Dale Evans
Paul and Linda McCartney

AND MUSICAL CHILDREN OF MUSICAL PARENTS

Nancy Sinatra and Frank Sinatra Jr.
Natalie Cole, daughter of Nat King Cole
Jakob Dylan, son of Bob
Liza Minnelli, daughter of Judy Garland
Hank Williams Jr. and Hank Williams III, son and grandson of Hank Williams
Arlo Guthrie, son of Woody Guthrie
Rufus Wainwright, son of Loudon Wainwright and Kate McGarrigle

MAMA DON'T ALLOW

TRACK 6

All right, backseat singers. This number is as close as it gets to the spirit of putting up a sign saying, No Parents Allowed! An American roots favorite that's a bit of a chameleon, "Mama Don't Allow" suits Texas country blues, or New Orleans–style jazz, or a bluegrass idiom, or pure sing-around-the-campfire high jinks, depending on who's playing it. And seemingly everyone likes singing about something that Mama doesn't allow, from guitar playing to cigar chewing. The carioke version is a rollicking arrangement full of wah-wahhing trumpets and a growling sax, whistles, cowbells, blocks, and honky-tonk piano. The lyrics are equally boisterous. Take a few turns, then encourage the grown-ups to make up their own version— "Kids don't allow . . ."

MAMA DON'T ALLOW
New lyrics by David Schiller.

Mama don't allow no backseat bickering here,
Mama don't allow no backseat bickering here,
We don't care what Mama don't allow,
Gonna bicker in the backseat anyhow,
Mama don't allow no backseat bickering here.

Piano solo

Mama don't allow no backseat bouncing here,
Mama don't allow no backseat bouncing here,
We don't care what Mama don't allow,
Gonna bounce in the backseat anyhow,
Mama don't allow no backseat bouncing here.

Guitar solo

Mama don't allow no backseat burping here.
Mama don't allow no backseat burping here.
We don't care what Mama don't allow,
Gonna burp in the backseat anyhow,
Mama don't allow no backseat burping here.

Saxophone solo

Mama don't allow no backseat back-talking here.
Mama don't allow no backseat back-talking here.
We don't care what Mama don't allow,
Gonna talk back in the backseat anyhow,
Mama don't allow no backseat back-talking here.

Trumpet solo

Repeat first verse

Symphony of Steel

What do calypso, limbo, and steel drum have in common? They all come from Trinidad. Begun in the 1930s, this innovative instrument is literally fashioned out of an oil drum. First the top is cut off—it's called the pan—then it's beaten into a concave shape. Raised areas are hammered in different shapes and sizes, which produce musical tones. Players make sound by hitting the pan with rubber-tipped mallets and, through ingenious arrangements, are capable of playing in all sorts of musical styles. Some steel bands have twenty or more members.

DAY-O (BANANA BOAT SONG)

TRACK 7

The infectious Caribbean beat of calypso first hit ears in the U.S. with the Andrews Sisters' 1944 version of Lord Invader's hit "Rum and Coca-Cola." But that was nothing compared to what happened a decade later when Harry Belafonte recorded "Day-O." That song appeared on Belafonte's album *Calypso*. Released in 1956, it was the first album ever to sell more than a million copies. Now there's something to sing about!

To get into the spirit of "Banana Boat Song," just imagine the feeling of swaying—swaying in a boat, or under a hammock, or swaying like palm trees on a sleepy beach. Then imagine your voice in a softly swaying arc, slow in the middle, quick at the end. And don't forget to put a punch in "BUNCH."

DAY-O (BANANA BOAT SONG)
Day me say day-o. *(Daylight come and me wan' go home.)*
Day me say day-o. *(Daylight come and me wan' go home.)*

Come, Mr. Tally Mon,
Tally me banana. *(Daylight come and me wan' go home.)*
Come, Mr. Tally Mon,
Tally me banana. *(Daylight come and me wan' go home.)*

It's six foot, seven foot,
Eight foot, BUNCH! *(Daylight come and me wan' go home.)*
It's six foot, seven foot,
Eight foot, BUNCH! *(Daylight come and me wan' go home.)*

Day me say day-o. *(Daylight come and me wan' go home.)*
Day me say day-o. *(Daylight come and me wan' go home.)*

A beautiful bunch
A ripe banana *(Daylight come and me wan' go home.)*
Hide the deadly
Black tarantula. *(Daylight come and me wan' go home.)*

It's six foot, seven foot,
Eight foot, BUNCH! *(Daylight come and me wan' go home.)*
It's six foot, seven foot,
Eight foot, BUNCH! *(Daylight come and me wan' go home.)*

Day me say day-o. *(Daylight come and me wan' go home.)*
Day me say day-o. *(Daylight come and me wan' go home.)*

MIGHTY CALYPSO

Calypso is the traditional carnival music of Trinidad, traceable back to the arrival of African slaves who were brought to work the sugar plantations. Starting in the early years of this century, tents were set up in Port of Spain, the island's capital, and every year between Christmas and Lent, calypso singers would vie for the best new song, with the winner declared "king." The competitions continue today, with lyrics like oral newspapers, full of commentary on the passing social and political scene. Professional calypsonians take on grandiose names like The Growling Tiger, Attila the Hun, Mighty Sparrow, Lord Kitchener, and Calypso Rose, the undisputed "Queen of Calypso."

Come, Mr. Tally Mon,
Tally me banana. *(Daylight come and me wan' go home.)*
Come, Mr. Tally Mon,
Tally me banana. *(Daylight come and me wan' go home.)*

It's six foot, seven foot,
Eight foot, BUNCH! *(Daylight come and me wan' go home.)*
It's six foot, seven foot,
Eight foot, BUNCH! *(Daylight come and me wan' go home.)*

Day me say day-o. *(Daylight come and me wan' go home.)*
Day me say day-o. *(Daylight come and me wan' go home.)*
(Daylight come and me wan' go home.)
(Daylight come and me wan' go home.)
(Daylight come and me wan' go—home!)

AYE, MATEYS!

Here are two traditional sea shanties. These were sung to help the crew get through the brutally hard work of running a full-fledged sailing ship. In a shanty, the "chanter" calls out the main lyrics and the men would back the chorus. You may know different words to both of these songs—dozens of versions exist.

"3x" means to sing the line three times.
"Early" should be pronounced "earl-eye."

DRUNKEN SAILOR
Chorus:
Way, hay up she rises (3x)
Early in the morning.
What will we do with a drunken sailor? (3x)
Early in the morning.

Verse:
Put him in a boat and row him over (3x)
Early in the morning.
Hoist him up to the topsail yardarm (3x)
Early in the morning.
Hoist him aboard with a running bowline (3x)
Early in the morning.
Shave his belly with a rusty razor (3x)
Early in the morning.

Way, hay up she rises(3x)
Early in the morning.
That's what you do with a drunken sailor (3x)
Early in the morning.

BLOW THE MAN DOWN
As I was a-walking down Paradise Street,
Way! Hey! Blow the man down!
A pretty young damsel I wanted to meet,
Gimme some time to blow the man down.

I says to her, "Polly, and how d'ye do?"
Way! Hey! Blow the man down!
She says, "None the better for seeing of you!"
Oh gimme some time to blow the man down.

All ye sailors take warning before you set sail,
Way! Hey! Blow the man down!
If he's strong as an ox and big as a whale,
Think twice before you blow the man down.

TRACK 8

WE'VE GOT RHYTHM

There are many rhythm games. Here's one that's quick and fun to play. Designate one person in the car as the rhythm master. That person lightly claps a beat to keep time. Then everyone else in the car takes turns speaking their full name in rhythm. Then go around the car designating a new person as the rhythm master, with a new beat to match!

BACKSEAT BOOGIE-WOOGIE

All right, singers, it's time to give the drummer some. Although long drum solos have become clichés in live rock performance, the drum drives the music along its rhythmic track. And no rhythm means no music. Try this: put your hand over the left side of your chest, as you may do when standing to sing "The Star-Spangled Banner." Feel it? That's your heartbeat, of course. And that's what drums are to music.

Now if you've skipped ahead and listened to "Backseat Boogie-Woogie" on the CD, you may be wondering where the words are. Well, there aren't any. Instead of singing to this one, we're going to drum to it. One way is to try to play along beat by beat. Another way is to create a kind of rhythmic "harmony"—while the drummer's rat-a-tat-tatting at lightning speed, you can be double-thumping every other main beat.

One thing to keep in mind: this activity gets better and more fun every time you try it.

How to Turn Your Car into a Drum Kit

No, even if you had them, you can't drag a bass drum, tom-toms, snare, and cymbals into your car. And you don't need to! Your vehicle is a fully equipped rhythm-mobile, and your hands and feet are the sticks. Slap the seat between your legs. That's one noise. Stomp on the floor—there's a very different type of noise.

For carioke purposes, we've simplified the range of drum tones into low, like the bass drum; medium, like the tom-toms; and high, like the snare and cymbals. Drummers layer these ranges together, which is what we'll try to do. Here's a rough guide to get you started:

Low • The low, or bass, usually provides the steady backbeat of a song. Two areas of the car that often provide a good bassy sound are the floor, which you can pound on with your foot, and the ceiling, which you can punch or slap lightly with your hand.

Medium • Where are your tom-toms? Most of the soft surfaces around you will provide a mid-range sound—the seat you're sitting on (spread legs slightly and start tapping the upholstery) and, if you're in the backseat or the way-back, the back of the seat in front of you, particularly the headrest. Careful, though—you don't want to start drumming on the driver's head! Windows also work to give a strong, medium sound.

High • For a crisp, "ping-y" sound, you need a taut surface, such as the hard plastic found on many door frames and dashboards. Other ways to achieve this sound include slapping on your knees, clapping, and, if you're really good at it, finger snapping.

DRUMROLL, PLEASE!

Dig that drumming? Check out Buddy Rich, Gene Krupa, Elvin Jones, and Billy Cobham. Some other famous drummers and their celebrated solos include:

Keith Moon, The Who
• "My Generation"

Michael Shrieve, Santana
• "Soul Sacrifice" (Woodstock performance)

John Bonham, Led Zeppelin • "Moby Dick"

Ringo Starr, The Beatles
• "The End"

Ginger Baker, Cream
• "Toad"

And, of course, Ron Bushy, Iron Butterfly • "Inna Gadda da Vida"

MARIACHI AND ITS INSTRUMENTS

The origins of mariachi are lost in time, but by the nineteenth century, there were two distinct mariachi cultures in Mexico, each using a different mixture of instruments. By the early twentieth century they merged. The biggest boost to mariachi came through sound recording and use in films in the 1940s and 1950s. Then in the late 1980s, Linda Ronstadt gave a huge American lift to mariachi with her album *Canciones de Mi Padre*. Mariachi ensembles vary depending on the musicians available, but the ideal instrumentation includes six violins, two trumpets, the guitar, the *vihuela*, and the *guitarrón*.

CIELITO LINDO

TRACK **9**

This traditional Mexican folk song has been a Spanish-language favorite for years. Even if the title is unfamiliar, as soon as the chorus begins with its infectious "¡Ay, ay, ay, ay!," you should find yourself immediately in the swing of it. The first bit of fun will be trying to sing in Spanish, lining up the syllables with the flow of the melody. And your second challenge is giving feeling to words whose meaning may be indecipherable!

CIELITO LINDO

First verse:
De la sierra morena,
Cielito lindo, vienen bajando
Un par de ojitos negros
Cielito lindo de contrabando.

Chorus:
¡Ay, ay, ay, ay!
Canta y no llores,
Porque cantando se alegran
Cielito lindo los corazones.

Second verse:

Una flecha en el aire
Cielito lindo lanzó Cupido
Y como fué jugando,
Cielito lindo, yo fuí el herido.

Repeat chorus

Instrumental

Repeat chorus

LOVELY HEAVEN

Roughly translated, *cielito lindo* means "lovely heaven," though in the context of the song it can simply mean "love"—as in, "Hello, love." Here is a simple translation of "Cielito Lindo," useful only for meaning and not intended to be sung:

From the mountain ranges, love, comes softly stealing
A pair of black eyes, love, that are being smuggled.

Ay, ay, ay, ay, sing and don't cry,
Because singing, love, gladdens the heart.

An arrow in the air, love, Cupid threw
And as it went playing, love, I was the wounded one.

VIHUELA: This five-string instrument with a belly in the back gives mariachi its unique sound, since no other genre of music uses a *vihuela*.

THE GUITARRÓN: This enormous guitarlike instrument with a short neck and bass sound provides the heartbeat of a mariachi ensemble.

THE GUITARRA DE GOLPE: About three fourths the size of a standard guitar, the *guitarra de golpe* came into use in the 1500s, but was replaced in the 1940s by the guitar/*vihuela* combination. Now it's making a comeback through innovative tuning and playing.

RISE AND SHINE

Bring on the glory, glory. This old African American spiritual is today most familiar as a children's favorite. And for good reason. Filled with clever word play and a clap-happy rhythm, it tells the story of Noah's Ark with great energy and glee. No one in the car will be able to resist joining in.

As for the driver, safety considerations preclude clapping in unison with the rest of the gang. But nowhere does it say you can't honk the horn!

RISE AND SHINE

Chorus:

Rise and shine and give God the glory, glory
Rise and shine and give God the glory, glory
Rise and shine and (CLAP) give God the glory, glory
Children of the Lord.

DON'T MEAN A THING IF IT AIN'T GOT THAT SWING.

It's not always easy to explain musical concepts with words, particularly when it comes to rhythm. But "Rise and Shine" is a classic example of syncopation. Syncopation is most simply defined as what happens when the accent is shifted from a beat that's normally strong to a beat that's normally weak. Syncopated rhythm can also be thought of as "offbeat." Syncopation shakes music up; it creates interest and variety. Now listen

First verse:

The Lord said to Noah:
There's gonna be a floody, floody.
The Lord said to Noah:
There's gonna be a floody, floody.
Get those children
Out (CLAP) of the muddy, muddy,
Children of the Lord.

Chorus:

Rise and shine and give God the glory, glory
Rise and shine and give God the glory, glory
Rise and shine and (CLAP) give God the glory, glory
Children of the Lord.

Piano solo

Second verse:

The Lord told Noah
To build him an arky, arky.
The Lord told Noah
To build him an arky, arky.
Build it out
Of (CLAP) hick'ry barky, barky,
Children of the Lord.

Repeat chorus

again to the music of "Rise and Shine," and see if you can pick up the syncopation. For example, try counting one-two-three-four or snapping your fingers over the music. You'll soon find yourself counting one-TWO-three-FOUR or snapping on the upbeat. Syncopation has been an important element in music since the Middle Ages, but it's absolutely integral to ragtime and jazz.

SIGN LANGUAGE

Using your hands to act out a song goes back to earliest childhood. The simplest is "Open, Shut Them"—hands out, palms forward on "open," then drawn and made into a fist on "shut them." Other favorites include the "Incy, Wincy Spider," with its climbing fingers, and "Wheels on the Bus," with its swish-swish-swish and move-on-back. The natural evolution of all these gestures—air guitar!

HAND JIVE

Hands up, to "rise." Fingers down, like the shining rays of the sun. And wave, wave, wave for glory. Here are the classic hand motions that make "Rise and Shine" even more fun to sing!

Rise and shine and give God the glor-y, glor-y!
Rise and shine and give God the glor-y, glor-y!

Rise and shine and (CLAP) give God the glor-y, glor-y!

Child-ren—of—the Lord!

Wiggle fingers over head on the last line.

Repeat these motions for each verse or make up new motions to match the words.

ADDITIONAL LYRICS FOR "RISE AND SHINE"

There are many verses to this song. Here are some more you can sing on your own.

He called for the animals,
They came in by twosie, twosies.
(Repeat)
Elephants and
Kang (CLAP) -a-roosie, roosies,
Children of the Lord.

It rained and it poured
For forty daysie, daysies.
(Repeat)
Almost drove
Those (CLAP) animals crazy, crazies,
Children of the Lord.

Noah he sent out
He sent out a dovey, dovey.
(Repeat)
Dovey said,
"There's (CLAP) clear skies abovey-bovey,"
Children of the Lord.

The sun came out and
It dried up the landy, landy.
(Repeat)
Everything
Was (CLAP) fine and dandy, dandy,
Children of the Lord.

The animals they came off
They came off by three-sie, three-sies.
(Repeat)
Grizzly bears
And (CLAP) chimpanzee-sie, zee-sies,
Children of the Lord.

That is the end of,
The end of my story, story.
(Repeat)
Everything (CLAP) is hunky dory, dory,
Children of the Lord.

GOSPEL SING-ALONG

Testify! Joyful or sorrowful, gospel songs are packed with powerful feeling, and should be sung that way. Try a few of these when you're in the mood, and your car will become a rolling revival meeting.

AMAZING GRACE

Amazing grace! How sweet the sound
That saved a wretch like me
I once was lost but now am found,
Was blind but now I see.

'Twas grace that taught my heart to fear
And grace my fears relieved
How precious did that grace appear
The hour I first believed.

Through many dangers, toils and snares
I have already come
'Tis grace that brought me safe thus far
And grace will lead me home.

When we've been there ten thousand years
Bright shining as the sun
We've no less days to sing God's praise
Than when we first begun.

NOBODY KNOWS THE TROUBLE I'VE SEEN

Nobody knows the trouble I've seen,
Nobody knows but Jesus.
Nobody knows the trouble I've seen,
Glory Hallelujah!

Sometimes I'm up,
Sometimes I'm down,
Oh, yes, Lord;
Sometimes I'm almost
To the ground,
Oh, yes, Lord.

I never shall
Forget that day,
Oh, yes, Lord.
When Jesus washed
My sins away,
Oh, yes, Lord.

HE'S GOT THE WHOLE WORLD IN HIS HANDS

He's got the whole world in His hands,
(Repeat twice)
He's got the whole world in His hands.

He's got the wind and the rain in His hands,
(Repeat twice)
He's got the whole world in His hands.

He's got the tiny little baby in His Hands,
(Repeat twice)
He's got the whole world in His hands.

He's got you and me, brother, in His hands,
(Repeat twice)
He's got the whole world in His hands.

GO TELL IT ON THE MOUNTAIN

Chorus:
Go, tell it on the mountain,
Over the hills and everywhere.
Go, tell it on the mountain,
That Jesus Christ is born.

While shepherds kept their watching
Over silent flocks by night
Behold throughout the heavens
There shone a holy light.

Repeat Chorus

SWING LOW, SWEET CHARIOT

Swing low, sweet chariot,
Comin' for to carry me home,
O swing low, sweet chariot,
Comin' for to carry me home.

I looked over Jordan and what did I see?
Comin' for to carry me home,
A band of angels comin' after me
Comin' for to carry me home.

If you get there before I do,
Comin' for to carry me home,
Tell all of my friends I'm comin' too,
Comin' for to carry me home.

ROCKETS' RED GLARE

It was toward the end of the War of 1812. For twenty-five hours the British pounded Baltimore's Fort McHenry. But when the smoke cleared, an enormous flag—a "star-spangled banner"—was still proudly flying. Inspired by this sight, a gifted amateur poet and hymnist named Francis Scott Key scribbled some notes for a poem on the back of an envelope. Back in Baltimore, he wrote out the

THE STAR-SPANGLED BANNER

TRACK ⓫

Ladies and gentlemen, please rise—but don't take off your seat belts! Do you think you can sing "The Star-Spangled Banner" by heart? Written by Francis Scott Key in 1814 and officially adopted as America's national anthem in 1931, the song is played at school assemblies, on military occasions, and, most familiarly, before sporting events. It raises a tear in the eye of many who hear it— and flutters in the stomach for many who have to sing it. Especially a cappella, before a huge stadium crowd. The melody has some truly challenging leaps, both up and down the scale, and there's always that moment toward the end when the crowd is holding its breath to see if the singer can hit the high note on "land of the free"—though these days, many performers like to push that note even higher, with a "free-*eeeeeeeeeee!*" See what you can do. Then pass the imaginary microphone to the next person in the car.

THE STAR-SPANGLED BANNER
Oh, say can you see,
By the dawn's early light,
What so proudly we hailed
At the twilight's last gleaming?
Whose broad stripes and bright stars
Through the perilous fight,

O'er the ramparts we watched
Were so gallantly streaming?
And the rockets' red glare
The bombs bursting in air
Gave proof through the night
That our flag was still there
Oh, say does that star-spangled
Banner yet wave—
O'er the land of the free
And the home of the brave!

A BANNER SPANGLED WITH FIFTEEN STARS

On June 14, 1777 (a date we now celebrate as Flag Day), Congress stipulated that the flag of the United States have thirteen alternate red and white stripes, with thirteen stars—white on a blue field—representing "a new constellation." The thirteen, of course, stand for the original thirteen colonies. The flag that flew over Fort McHenry, christened the "star-spangled banner" by Francis Scott Key, had fifteen stars and fifteen stripes—representing two new states. Then in 1818, with the addition of five more states to the Union, Congress again changed the design back to thirteen stripes. There were twenty stars, with the provision that an additional star be added for each new state.

four verses and almost immediately the poem was printed as a broadside, with Key's suggestion that it should be sung to the then popular British melody, "To Anacreon in Heaven." Within a month, the broadside appeared in newspapers up and down the East Coast. Soon after, a Baltimore music store published the words and music together as "The Star-Spangled Banner." The song grew steadily more popular; by the time the Civil War had started, it was played on most patriotic occasions, although it would not be made America's national anthem for another seventy years.

AN AMERICANA SONG SAMPLER

Now that you've gotten in the mood with "The Star-Spangled Banner," keep the red-white-and-blue mood going with these sing-along favorites.

AMERICA THE BEAUTIFUL

Katherine Lee Bates was inspired to write the poem "America the Beautiful" after a trip to the top of Pikes Peak, Colorado, in 1893.

O beautiful for spacious skies,
For amber waves of grain,
For purple mountain majesties
Above the fruited plain!

America! America!
God shed His grace on thee,
And crown thy good with brotherhood
From sea to shining sea!

O beautiful for pilgrim feet
Whose stern impassion'd stress
A thoroughfare for freedom beat
Across the wilderness.

O beautiful for heroes prov'd
In liberating strife,
Who more than self their country loved,
And mercy more than life.

O beautiful for patriot dream
That sees beyond the years
Thine alabster cities gleam
Undimmed by human tears.

America! America!
God shed his grace on thee,
And crown thy good with brotherhood
From sea to shining sea.

TAKE ME OUT TO THE BALL GAME

This is the second most widely sung song in America, after "The Star-Spangled Banner." And, curiously, with lyrics and music by two men who at the time (1908) had never been to a baseball game!

Take me out to the ball game,
Take me out with the crowd.
Buy me some peanuts and Cracker Jack,
I don't care if I never get back,
Let me root, root, root for the home team,
If they don't win it's a shame.
For it's one, two, three strikes, you're out,
At the old ball game.

YOU'RE A GRAND OLD FLAG

*This rousing patriotic number was written
by George M. Cohan, who also wrote
"Give My Regards to Broadway."*

You're a grand old flag,
You're a high flying flag
And forever in peace may you wave.
You're the emblem of
The land I love.
The home of the free and the brave.

Ev'ry heart beats true
'neath the Red, White and Blue,
Where there's never a boast or brag.
Should auld acquaintance be forgot,
Keep your eye on the grand old flag.

MY COUNTRY 'TIS OF THEE ("AMERICA")

My country 'tis of thee,
Sweet land of liberty,
Of thee I sing.
Land where my fathers died!
Land of the Pilgrim's pride!
From every mountain side,
Let freedom ring!

Let music swell the breeze,
And ring from all the trees
Sweet freedom's song.
Let mortal tongues awake;
Let all that breathe partake;
Let rocks their silence break,
The sound prolong.

Our father's God, to Thee,
Author of liberty,
To Thee we sing.
Long may our land be bright
With freedom's holy light;
Protect us by Thy might,
Great God, our King!

HOW HITS ARE BORN

Arlo Guthrie was playing a gig in Chicago in 1971. After the show, he was approached by a then unknown songwriter named Steve Goodman, who had some songs he thought Arlo should record. Arlo, who got this kind of request often, asked Steve to buy him a beer and said he would listen to Steve's songs for as long as the beer would last. Goodman played "City of New Orleans"— and Arlo made him buy him another beer! The following year Arlo Guthrie released the song on a record called *Hobo's Lullaby*, and it became a Top 20 hit and the pinnacle of his career.

THE CITY OF NEW ORLEANS

Written by Steve Goodman, a "songwriter's songwriter," this poignant song of a train trip through main street America became a major hit for Arlo Guthrie, Willie Nelson, and Johnny Cash. Sing it straight, like a storyteller, with a wistful quaver. The mood of the song reflects a time when half the passenger trains in America were about to disappear. But *The City of New Orleans* thrives today, leaving Union Station in Chicago daily at 8:00 P.M. And "The City of New Orleans" joins "Casey Jones," "Orange Blossom Special," and "Wabash Cannonball" as a classic American train song.

THE CITY OF NEW ORLEANS
Words and music by Steve Goodman,
Turnpike Tom Music/Jurisdad Music (ASCAP)
All rights reserved. Used by permission.

First verse:
Riding on The City of New Orleans,
Illinois Central Monday morning rail.
Fifteen cars and fifteen restless riders,
Three conductors and twenty-five sacks of mail.

All along the southbound odyssey
The train pulls out at Kankakee
And rolls along past houses, farms and fields.
Passin' trains that have no names,
Freight yards full of old black men
And the graveyards of the rusted automobiles.

Chorus:

Good morning America how are you?
Said, Don't you know me I'm your native son,
I'm the train they call The City of New Orleans,
I'll be gone five hundred miles when the day is done.

Second verse:

Dealin' card games with the old men in the club car.
Penny a point ain't no one keepin' score.
Pass the paper bag that holds the bottle
Feel the wheels rumblin' 'neath the floor.
And the sons of Pullman porters
And the sons of engineers
Ride their fathers' magic carpets
    made of steel.
Mothers with their babes asleep,
Are rockin' to the gentle beat
And the rhythm of the rails is all they feel.

ALL ABOARD FOR . . .

"The City of New Orleans" tells the story of a passenger train that goes from Chicago to the Big Easy. Can you match the Amtrak trains with their routes?

1. *Sunset Limited*
2. *Texas Eagle*
3. *Empire Builder*
4. *Coast Starlight*
5. *Crescent*
6. *Silver Service*
7. *Ethan Allen Express*
8. *California Zephyr*

a. Seattle to Los Angeles
b. New York to Rutland
c. Chicago to San Francisco
d. New York to New Orleans
e. Chicago to San Antonio
f. Orlando to Los Angeles
g. Chicago to Seattle
   or Portland
h. New York to Tampa,
   or Miami

Answers: 1-f, 2-e, 3-g, 4-a, 5-d, 6-h, 7-b, 8-c.

Repeat chorus

Third verse:
Nighttime on The City of New Orleans,
Changing cars in Memphis, Tennessee.
Halfway home, we'll be there by morning
Through the Mississippi darkness
Rolling down to the sea.
But all the towns and people seem
To fade into a bad dream
And the steel rail still ain't heard the news.
The conductor sings his songs again,
The passengers will please refrain
This train's got the disappearing railroad
   blues.

Chorus:
Good night America how are you?
Said, Don't you know me I'm your native son,
I'm the train they call The City of New Orleans,
I'll be gone five hundred miles when
   the day is done.

PLANES, TRAINS, AND AUTOMOBILES

Musicians have had a long love affair with the open road. See if you can match the song title and the artist(s) who made it famous with the form of transportation that it celebrates.

- "Leaving on a Jet Plane," Peter, Paul and Mary
- "America," Paul Simon
- "Ol' 55," The Eagles/Tom Waits
- "Radar Love," Golden Earring
- "Back in the USSR," the Beatles
- "Pink Cadillac," Bruce Springsteen
- "Magic Bus," the Who
- "Coming into Los Angeles," Arlo Guthrie
- "The Letter," the Boxtops
- "She'll Be Coming Round the Mountain," traditional
- "Homeward Bound," Simon and Garfunkel
- "Rollin' in My Sweet Baby's Arms," Leon Russell/Flatt and Scruggs/Willie Nelson, et al.
- "Wabash Cannonball," Carter Family/ Johnny Cash, et al.
- "Born to Run," Bruce Springsteen

- "Downtown Train," Tom Waits/Rod Stewart
- "Maybelline," Chuck Berry
- "Convoy," C. W. McCall
- "King of the Road," Roger Miller
- "409"
- "Little Deuce Coupe"
- "Born to Be Wild," Steppenwolf
- "Big Yellow Taxi," Joni Mitchell
- "Casey Jones," the Grateful Dead et al.
- "No Expectations," the Rolling Stones
- "Rock Island Line," Leadbelly, the Weavers, et al.

Answers (in order): plane, bus, car, car, plane, car, bus, plane, plane, train, bus, train, train, motorcycle, subway, car, truck, train, car, car, motorcycle, taxi, train, train and plane, train.

RED RIVER VALLEY

TRACK 13

All right, here's a test of interpretive prowess: can you put enough feeling into the line "And the cowboy who loved you so true" to make your horse weep? All kidding aside, this sentimental Western favorite actually began life as a popular parlor song written about upstate New York. So while it feels as timeless as the prairie, it's not. For the big and little cowboys in the car, the fun comes in choosing whether to sing the song in the upbeat style of the Riders of the Sky (like Ranger Doug, Woody Paul, and Too Slim), or with the raspy voice of a Gabby Hayes, or stoically, like a young Gary Cooper. And for all the cowgirls in the car, it's easy enough to flip the song by pining about "the cowgirl who loved you so true."

RED RIVER VALLEY

First verse:
From this valley they say you are going
We will miss your bright eyes and sweet smile
For they say you are taking the sunshine
That has brightened our pathways awhile.

Chorus:

Come and sit by my side, if you love me
Do not hasten to bid me adieu
Just remember the Red River Valley
And the cowboy who loved you so true.

Fiddle solo

Second verse:

Won't you think of the valley you're leaving
Oh how lonely, how sad it will be?
Oh think of the kind hearts you're breaking
And the grief you are causing to me.

Chorus:

Come and sit by my side, if you love me
Do not hasten to bid me adieu
Just remember the Red River Valley
And the cowboy who loved you so true.

AT LEAST TWO RED RIVER VALLEYS

A northern Red River Valley runs between Minnesota and North Dakota and into Manitoba, Canada. A southwestern Red River Valley ranges along the Texas-Oklahoma border. A number of versions of the song exist, including some with many more stanzas, and they reflect these two different regions.

GATHER 'ROUND THE CAMPFIRE

You can just picture it. The end of the day. A couple of weary cowpokes are resting their tired bones on logs and bedrolls. The campfire's burning, coffee's brewing, the beans are cooking. From a distance comes the gentle lowing of cattle, and the sound of a far-off coyote. Then one young hand pulls out a harmonica and starts to play a slow, wistful strain of "Red River Valley." Sweet.

If you have a harmonica around the house, bring it on your next trip and you could be serenading your family just like the musical cowhand. Here's a quick lesson on getting started, and easy tablature for the song.

1. Hold the harmonica between your two hands with the numbers facing up, putting "1" on the left. If you don't have numbers on your harmonica, blow through the notes. The lowest note should be on the left. Also, the harmonica should actually be inside your mouth, not just on the lips.

2. Practice blowing through one hole to make a single note. If you have a C harmonica— the most common—blow through the 4 hole. Voilà, a C. If you're not getting a clean, one-note sound, it might help in the beginning to cover holes 3 and 5 with your index fingers.

3. Then practice drawing a breath, or inhaling, through a single hole. Draw on the 4 hole, and that's a D. Then practice "bending" a note. This is a trick harmonica players use to change the pitch. The easiest way to bend a note is to tilt the harmonica toward your nose while blowing, then listen as the note gets lower and lower.

4. Finally, to achieve a tremolo effect (for example, on the words "going," "smile," "sunshine" and "awhile" in the first verse), practice holding the harmonica with your hands forming a kind of cup around it. Then flutter the hand cupping the back of the harmonica, and listen as the sound wavers musically.

5. So here goes! And remember, this gets easier and easier with a little bit of practice.

Remember that the number refers to the hole in the harmonica, and that "B" means to blow and "D" means to draw. Have fun!

Red River Valley

3B 4B 5B 5B 5B 5B 4D 5B 4D 4B 3B 4B
5B 4D 5B 6B 5D 5B 4D 6B 5D 5B 5B 4D
4B 4D 5B 6B 5D 3D 3D 3B 3D 4B 4D 5B
4D 4D

Here are a few more beginner's songs to play on the harmonica. In fact, you may find them a bit easier than "Red River Valley."

On Top of Old Smokey

4B 4B 5B 6B 7B 6D
6D 5D 6B 6D 6B

4B 4B 5B 6B 6B 4D
5B 5D 5B 4D 4B

Twinkle, Twinkle Little Star

4B 4B 6B 6B 6D 6D 6B
5D 5D 5B 5B 4D 4D 4B

6B 6B 5D 5D 5B 5B 4D
6B 6B 5D 5D 5B 5B 4D

4B 4B 6B 6B 6D 6D 6B
5D 5D 5B 5B 4D 4D 4B

Happy Birthday

6B 6B 6D 6B 7B 7D
6B 6B 6D 6B 8D 7B

6B 6B 9B 8B 7B 7D 6D
9D 9D 8B 7B 8D 7B

Kum Ba Yah

4B 5B 6B 6B 6B 6D 6D 6B
4B 5B 6B 6B 6B 5D 5B 4D

4B 5B 6B 6B 6B 6D 6D 6B
5D 5B 4B 4D 4D 4B

Clementine

4B 4B 4B 3B 5B 5B 5B 4B
4B 5B 6B 6B 5D 5B 4D

4D 5B 5D 5D 5B 4D 5B 4B
4B 5B 4D 3B 3D 4D 4B

45

"LADIES AND
GENTLEMEN,
MY MOTHER
THANKS YOU,
MY FATHER
THANKS YOU,
MY SISTER
THANKS YOU,
AND I THANK
YOU!"

—GEORGE M. COHAN'S
SIGNATURE SIGN-OFF

GIVE MY REGARDS TO BROADWAY

TRACK 14

Break out your straw boaters and bamboo canes! This song is Broadway's national anthem. Fittingly, it was written by a man who once "owned" Broadway—George M. Cohan, a creative dynamo in the development of American popular theater. "Give My Regards to Broadway" appeared in Cohan's breakout production of 1904, *Little Johnny Jones*. Also from the same show came a little number called "Yankee Doodle Boy," known forever after as "Yankee Doodle Dandy."

Put on your best song-and-dance voice. Stretch those vowels. Ham it up! Our carioke version is brisk and happy, and full of the sounds of a much more innocent time.

P.S.: For extra fun, take your emergency flashlight from the glove compartment— you *do* have an emergency flashlight in the glove compartment, don't you?—and use it to spotlight the backseat singers.

GIVE MY REGARDS TO BROADWAY

Give my regards to Broadway.
Remember me to Herald Square.
Tell all the gang at Forty-second Street
That I will soon be there.
Whisper of how I'm yearning
To mingle with the old-time throng.
Give my regards to old Broadway
And say that I'll be there ere long!

Instrumental

Whisper of how I'm yearning
To mingle with the old-time throng.
Give my regards to Broadway
And say that I'll be there ere long.
Give my regards to old Broadway
And say that I'll be there ere long!

THE GREAT WHITE WAY

Broadway's first electric lights appeared on a theater marquee in 1891. Soon the theater district, spanning Thirteenth to Forty-fifth streets, was ablaze, earning its moniker the Great White Way. Today the primitive light bulbs have evolved into sophisticated video and space-age neon, and there are still few places in the world as lit up and eye-catching as Times Square. And if you're there for a show, check out the statue of George M. Cohan at Forty-sixth and Broadway.

THE PIPES, THE PIPES

Have fun with this one. Think of the melody as a gentle, octave-and-a-half ride from glen to glen. And think of your voice as a sweet Irish pipe, filling the valley with song. But watch out for the phrase "I'll be here in sunshine . . ." Between "be" and "here" is a leap of *four whole steps*. On the other hand, you can put on a brogue, pronouncing "and down" as "ah doon," for example. Once everyone gets the giggles out, let each member of the family take a turn pining away for Danny. If all goes well, there won't be a dry eye in the car.

DANNY BOY

TRACK 15

Is there a more beautiful, poignant song than "Danny Boy"? In fact, so lovely is the melody, sometimes still known as the "Londonderry Air," that more than 100 songs have been composed to it. Then in 1912, a prolific English songwriter (and lawyer!) named Frederic Edward Weatherly received a copy of the tune from his American sister-in-law. He'd been working unsuccessfully on a song called "Danny Boy," and this haunting music fit his lyrics perfectly. He published the song in 1913 and made magic. Virtually everyone has recorded "Danny Boy," from Elvis to Patti LaBelle, Judy Garland to Roy Orbison, Andy Williams, Glenn Miller, Jackie Wilson, Tony Bennett, Patti Paige, the Chieftains, Johnny Cash, Joan Baez, Bing Crosby— the list goes on and on, topping 200.

DANNY BOY

Verse:

Oh Danny boy, the pipes, the pipes are calling;
From glen to glen, and down the mountain side.
The summer's gone, and all the roses falling,
It's you, it's you must go and I must bide.

Chorus:

But come you back when summer's in the meadow,
Or when the valley's hushed and white with snow,
'Tis I'll be here in sunshine or in shadow.
Oh, Danny boy,
Oh, Danny boy,
I love you so.

Pennywhistle solo

Chorus:

But come you back when summer's in the meadow,
Or when the valley's hushed and white with snow.
'Tis I'll be here in sunshine or in shadow.
Oh, Danny boy,
Oh, Danny boy,
I love you so.

DANNY, WE HARDLY KNEW YE

Who is the "I" singing to Danny? One theory has it that the song's protagonist is an Irish chieftain bidding farewell to his youngest son, who is going into battle. Another is that Danny is leaving Ireland during the famine, and this is his mother's lament. Another has Danny running off to join the IRA. And then there's a version from 1918, which instructs male singers to substitute the female name "Eily" for "Danny," casting it as a simple love song. So here's one idea to fill a lull in the trip: Make up your own story about Danny. Where is he going? Who is singing to him? And will the singer be alive when Danny returns?

TWELVE-BAR BLUES

Originally patterned after English ballads, the blues developed into a definite progression of eight, twelve, and sixteen measures or bars. The twelve-bar blues (with its I-I-I-I-IV-IV-I-I-V-V-I-I chord progression, for those who know music theory) is by far the most popular. As for the structure of the lyrics, that too is unique, with the songs traditionally made up of several three-line "call-and-response" verses. There the pattern is A-A-B.

ARE WE THERE YET BLUES

TRACK 16

ALL-AMERICAN CAR-I-OKE wouldn't be American without at least one blues song, because it was the blues, that most American of musical and verse forms, that influenced and defined American popular music. Out of the blues come country, jazz, and, especially, rock and roll. So our song journey ends with a classic twelve-bar blues.

On the other hand, ALL-AMERICAN CAR-I-OKE wouldn't be carioke without a fun activity, and "Are We There Yet Blues" takes its cue from the true spirit of the blues—improvisation. It's simple, and it's pure silliness. Here's how it works. Each line of verse has one or more blanks in it labeled by a letter. Below the verse are lists of words grouped by letter. Take a word from column A, and insert it when you come to the blank labeled A. Here's an example of a verse and how it works:

I woke up this morning, found a ___(A)___ in my shoes
I woke up this morning, found a ___(A)___ in my shoes
That ___(A)___ in my shoes
Gives me the ___(B)___ blues.

(A) building · jellyfish · mushroom · sock · spider · spitball
(B) cross-eyed · heebie-jeebie · highway · hungry · purple · thumping

So you might sing:
I woke up this morning, found a spider in my shoes
I woke up this morning, found a spider in my shoes
That spider in my shoes
Gives me the cross-eyed blues.

"Are We There Yet Blues" works like a contemporary blues song, with verses, a chorus, and a swinging instrumental and saxophone solo in the middle. Here are three verses and the chorus, each with suggested word substitutions. But feel free to be creative and choose your own words to add. Better yet, make up your own verses altogether.

ARE WE THERE YET BLUES
Lyrics by David Schiller.

Verse 1:

The backseat of this car smells like ___**(A)**___ underpants,
The backseat of this car smells like ___**(A)**___ underpants,
Those ___**(A)**___ underpants,
Make me wish I was ___**(B)**___.

(A) crusty · gorilla's · hairy · ice-cold · lacy · licorice · moldy · polka-dot · sandy · scratchy
(B) an ant · an elephant · at a dance · at a séance · in an ambulance · in a trance · in France · named Rembrandt

BLUE NOTE

Another distinguishing characteristic of the blues is the "bent pitch" or blue note, which sounds to most ears like a note out of tune. The blue note—a product of the marriage of African and Western musical systems—started with singers, but soon after musicians began experimenting with bent notes. Nowadays every rock guitarist knows how to bend a string to create a bluesy wail.

A BLUE HISTORY

The blues is uniquely American, a merging of West African and European music fomented in the south as slaves sang songs telling of their deep suffering. Taking shape after the Civil War, the blues evolved out of field hollers, ballads, dance and church music into a call-and-response between a singer and his guitar. (In the early days the blues was a decidedly masculine form.) The singer would sing. The guitar would answer. Just before World War I, a black composer named W. C. Handy popularized the blues with songs like "Memphis Blues" and "St. Louis Blues." The 1920s saw the blues become a national craze as— ironically—women singers like Bessie Smith led the way. Gradually the blues

Chorus:
I say when *(when?)*
When will we get there?
   (Are we there yet?)
   (We there yet?)
(Repeat)
My ____**(A)**____ is broke,
This ____**(B)**____ 's a joke,
We're ____**(C)**____, ____**(C)**____, ____**(C)**____, ____**(C)**____, ____**(C)**____ !

(A) butt · hope · mind · spirit · voice · will
(B) car · day · ride · trip
(C) blue · bored · giddy · lost · nuts · tired

Verse 2:
My ____**(A)**____ ____**(B)**____ 's the worst driver you ever saw,
My ____**(A)**____ ____**(B)**____ 's the worst driver you ever saw,
When my ____**(A)**____ ____**(B)**____ 's behind the wheel,
You better ____**(C)**____ the law.

(A) chattering · cross-eyed · dazed and confused · giggly · grouchy · jumpy · kindly old · lead-footed · oblivious · screaming · sensitive · tongue-tied

(B) aunt · big brother · big sister · mama · school bus driver · papa · uncle

(C) bribe · join up with · flag down · get used to · pray for · pretend you're · run from · say hello to · watch out for

Repeat chorus

Verse 3:

We stopped into a diner, ordered ___**(A)**__ to eat,
We stopped into a diner, ordered ___**(A)**__ to eat,
But once we ate our ___**(A)**__ ,
We ___**(B)**__ on our seat.

(A) beef brains · bile burgers · chicken feet · fish heads · garlic ice cream · gooey broccoli · gopher guts · gristle gumbo · ladybugs · night crawlers · rotten eggs · sandy salad · squirrel stew

(B) burst out laughing · did the rhumba · fell asleep · got jiggy · had a party · jumped up and down · keeled over · kissed the sky · lost our lunch · went crazy

Repeat chorus

traveled north with the migration of southern blacks. Soon there were thriving blues traditions in cities like Chicago and Detroit, and a new sound born of the electric guitar. By the 1960s, rock discovered its blues roots and revived it—again, ironically, as most of the blues flowed back into America from Britain, where it had been adopted by bands such as the Rolling Stones, Cream, and Led Zeppelin.

"Sumer Is Icumen In," the earliest round in English, appeared in the thirteenth or fourteenth century:

OLD ENGLISH

Sumer is icumen in,
Lhude sing cuccu!
Groweth sed, and bloweth
    med,
And springeth the wde nu.
Sing cuccu!
Awe bleteth after lomb,
Lhouth after calve cu;
Bulluc sterteth, bucks
    verteth,
Murie sing cuccu.
Cuccu, cuccu!
Wel singes thu cuccu,
Ne swik thu naver nu.

ROUND AND ROUND

Today when we think of musical rounds, the first to come to mind is usually "Row, Row, Row Your Boat" or "Frère Jacques." That's because since the beginning of the twentieth century, rounds have been used to teach children how to sing. But it wasn't always so. The round, also called a catch, is an English musical form—essentially a simple canon or fugue—that goes back at least to the fourteenth century, and has gathered a rich history around it over the centuries. Rounds celebrate all activities of life. There are rounds about friendship, love, work; sacred rounds and profane rounds; rounds as toasts and rounds as epitaphs; nonsense rounds and patriotic rounds. Catch clubs popped up all over England in the seventeenth and eighteenth centuries, the golden age of the round. Visiting musicians at the time were also intrigued, resulting in rounds written by Haydn, Mozart, Beethoven, Mendelssohn, Cherubini, and others.

Here are a few popular rounds, sung by a single voice on the disk. Then if you really get in the spirit, check out the music section at your local library for rounds collections. You'll probably need to know how to read music, as there are few commercial recordings of rounds available.

TRACK 17: Hear "Kookaburra" as a round with three singers.

(The lyrics are numbered for simplicity—when your first singer finishes line one and begins line two, the second singer starts line one, and so on.)

TRACK 18: KOOKABURRA

1. Kookaburra sits in the old gum tree
2. Merry merry king of the bush is he,
3. Laugh, kookaburra, laugh, kookaburra
4. Gay your life must be.

TRACK 19: WHITE CORAL BELLS

1. White coral bells upon a slender stalk
2. Lilies of the valley deck the garden walk.
3. Oh, don't you wish that you could hear them ring,
4. That will happen only when the fairies sing.

TRACK 20: HEY HO, NOBODY HOME

1. Hey, ho, nobody home,
2. Meat nor drink nor money have I none,
3. Yet, will I be merry!

TRACK 21: OH, HOW LOVELY IS THE EVENING

1. Oh, how lovely is the evening, is the evening,
2. When the bells are sweetly ringing, sweetly ringing,
3. Ding dong, ding dong, ding dong.

MODERN TRANSLATION

Summer is a-coming in,
Loudly sing cuckoo;
Groweth seed and bloweth
*   mead,*
And springeth wood anew.
Sing cuckoo!
Ewe bleateth after lamb,
Low'th after calf the cow;
Bullock started, buck to
*   fern go'th,*
Merry sing cuckoo!
Cuckoo, cuckoo!
Well singest thou cuckoo,
Nor cease thou ever now.

ACKNOWLEDGMENTS, CREDITS, AND BIG THANKS

Aᴌᴌ-Aᴍᴇʀɪᴄᴀɴ Cᴀʀ-ɪ-ᴏᴋᴇ is a simple idea that was complicated to produce, and it might never have happened without the fortuitous arrival of David Allender, who brought an extraordinary amount of energy, creativity, humor, and passion to the project. I can't thank him enough. Special thank-yous go also to Paul Hanson, for resuscitating the idea with a bold new design; Suzie Bolotin, for getting it immediately, pushing it forward, and singing, too; Wayne Kirn, for the ingenious packaging; Paul Gamarello, for the terrific look; Anne Cherry, for skillfully tending the words; Sophie Deutsch, for her excellent research and editorial help; Jim Eber, for enthusiastically planting seeds; all the people at Workman who sang "Proud Mary" in front of a somewhat stunned audience; and to Peter Workman, for taking a second look and saying yes without a moment's hesitation.

I also want to thank the Carioke Singers, whose talents are heard on Track 1: Suzie Bolotin, Andrew Mandel, Asa Miraglia, Suzanne Rafer, Lily Rothman, Clara, Quinn, and Theo Schiller, Jessica Swain, Carolan Workman, with a special thank-you to bass voice and choirmaster extraordinaire, Lloyd Mair. In addition to drumming, Charles de Montebello also recorded the sessions with reassuring patience. Please take a bow!